IGNITING THE SPARKS OF GENIUS

A Guideline to Launching and Sustaining a Successful Startup

CONTENTS

Foreword 3

Chapter 1: Finding Your Purpose: Discovering Your Passion and Defining Your Vision 4

Chapter 2: Overcoming Adversity: Navigating Obstacles and Staying Resilient 7

Chapter 3: Building a Strong Team: Attracting Top Talent and Fostering Collaboration 10

Chapter 4: Embracing Risk: Taking Calculated Chances and Making Bold Decisions 13

Chapter 5: Sustaining Success: Continuously Innovating and Staying Ahead of the Game 15

Chapter 6: Developing a Growth Mindset: Embracing Change and Continuous Learning 18

Chapter 7: Establishing Your Brand: Defining Your Unique Identity and Value Proposition 20

Chapter 8: Strategizing for Success: Creating a Winning Business Plan 22

Chapter 9: Securing Funding: Finding the Right Investors and Maximizing Resources 24

Chapter 10: Embracing Failure: Learning from Mistakes and Moving Forward 26

Summary 28

Final Message 32

Foreword

Starting a business can be one of the most challenging and rewarding experiences of your life. It requires hard work, determination, and a willingness to take risks and face challenges head-on. Yet, the rewards of entrepreneurship are many - the satisfaction of creating something from scratch, the thrill of turning your vision into reality, and the freedom and flexibility that come with being your own boss.

This book, "Igniting the Sparks of Genius: A Guide to Starting and Growing Your Startup," is a comprehensive guide for anyone looking to turn their entrepreneurial dream into a reality. It provides practical, actionable advice on the key elements of starting and growing a successful business, including finding your purpose, navigating adversity, building a strong team, embracing risk, and sustaining success.

Whether you're just starting out or looking to take your existing business to the next level, this book will provide you with the inspiration and guidance you need to succeed. From understanding your passion and defining your vision, to overcoming obstacles and making bold decisions, "Igniting the Sparks of Genius" will help you tap into the entrepreneurial spirit within you and unleash your full potential.

So, if you're ready to ignite the fire within, pick up this book and get started on your entrepreneurial journey today. You'll find the tools, insights, and inspiration you need to turn your dreams into reality and achieve the success you've always imagined.

Chapter 1: Finding Your Purpose - Discovering Your Passion and Defining Your Vision

Starting a new business is an exciting journey, but it can also be overwhelming and stressful. Before jumping into the world of entrepreneurship, it's essential to have a clear understanding of what drives you and what you want to achieve. This chapter will focus on finding your purpose and defining your vision, as these two elements will serve as the foundation for your startup.

Discovering Your Passion

The first step in finding your purpose is discovering your passion. Passion is what will keep you motivated and inspired during the ups and downs of starting a business. It's what will drive you to keep pushing forward when things get tough. Without passion, it's easy to lose sight of why you started your business in the first place.

One of the best ways to discover your passion is to reflect on what you love to do. What activities do you find yourself lost in for hours on end? What are your hobbies and interests? What skills do you possess that you're naturally good at? These are all clues that can help you uncover your passion.

Once you've identified your passions, you should explore ways to turn them into a business idea. For example, if you're passionate about cooking, you could start a food truck, open a restaurant, or launch a catering service. If you're passionate about fitness, you could start a personal training business, create a workout app, or open a gym.

Defining Your Vision

Once you've discovered your passion, the next step is to define your vision. Your vision is the end goal you want to achieve with your business. It's what you want to see when you look back on your journey years from now.

To define your vision, ask yourself the following questions:

- What impact do you want to have on the world with your business?

- What problems do you want to solve?
- What kind of lifestyle do you want to have as a result of your business?
- What kind of legacy do you want to leave?

Your vision should be specific, measurable, and attainable. It should inspire you and drive you forward. Write down your vision and put it somewhere you can see it every day.

Building a Strong Personal Foundation

Discovering your passion and defining your vision is just the beginning. You also need to build a strong personal foundation to help you navigate the challenges of starting a business. This includes developing a growth mindset, building self-awareness, and cultivating resilience.

A growth mindset is the belief that you can grow and improve through hard work and dedication. This mindset is essential for entrepreneurs because starting a business is not easy, and you will face many challenges along the way. With a growth mindset, you'll be more likely to embrace these challenges and learn from them, instead of getting discouraged and giving up.

Self-awareness is the ability to understand your strengths and weaknesses, and how they impact your thoughts, feelings, and behavior. Building self-awareness will help you identify your blind spots and work on them, so you can become a better leader and entrepreneur.

Resilience is the ability to bounce back from setbacks and adversity. As an entrepreneur, you will face many obstacles, and it's essential to have resilience to keep going. Building resilience can be done through mindfulness, exercise, and developing a strong support network.

Conclusion

Finding your purpose and defining your vision are crucial steps in starting a successful business. By discovering your passion and setting a clear vision, you'll have a roadmap to guide you on your journey. Building a strong personal foundation will help you navigate the challenges you'll face along the way. Remember, starting a business is not a sprint, but a marathon, and having a clear understanding of your purpose and vision, as well as a strong personal foundation, will help you stay motivated and focused on your goals. In the next chapters, we will dive deeper into overcoming adversity, building a strong team, embracing risk, and sustaining success. By following the principles outlined in this book, you'll be well on your way to launching and growing a successful startup. Remember to stay focused, stay resilient, and never lose sight of why you started this journey in the first place. With hard work, dedication, and a little bit of luck, you can achieve great things and make a positive impact in the world. So, take a deep breath, believe in yourself, and let's get started!

Chapter 2: Overcoming Adversity - Navigating Obstacles and Staying Resilient

Starting a business is an exciting journey, but it's also full of challenges and obstacles. As an entrepreneur, you need to be prepared to navigate these obstacles and stay resilient in the face of adversity. In this chapter, we'll explore some of the common challenges you'll face as a startup founder, and provide tips for overcoming them.

Managing Failure

One of the biggest obstacles entrepreneurs face is failure. Failure is inevitable in business, and it's something that every entrepreneur will experience at some point. It's important to understand that failure is not the end of the road, but a learning opportunity.

To overcome failure, you need to develop a growth mindset. A growth mindset is the belief that you can grow and improve through hard work and dedication. With a growth mindset, you'll be more likely to embrace failure as a learning opportunity, and use it to grow and improve.

You can also overcome failure by being persistent. Persistence is the key to success, and it's what will help you keep going when things get tough. Remember that success is not a straight line, but a journey with ups and downs. By staying persistent, you'll be able to overcome obstacles and achieve your goals.

Handling Rejection

Another common challenge entrepreneurs face is rejection. Whether it's a rejection from a potential customer, investor, or employee, rejection can be hard to handle. It's important to remember that rejection is a normal part of the entrepreneurial journey, and it's something that every entrepreneur will experience at some point.

To handle rejection, it's important to have a thick skin and not take things personally. Instead of dwelling on the rejection, use it as a learning opportunity. Ask for feedback and use it to improve your product or pitch. Remember that rejection is not a reflection of your worth as a person, but a part of the entrepreneurial journey.

Managing Stress and Burnout

Starting a business is stressful, and it's important to find ways to manage stress and prevent burnout. Stress and burnout can have a negative impact on your health, as well as your business.

To manage stress and prevent burnout, it's important to take care of yourself. This includes getting enough sleep, eating a balanced diet, and exercising regularly. It's also important to set boundaries and make time for yourself, so you can recharge and be at your best.

Another way to manage stress is to practice mindfulness. Mindfulness is the practice of being present in the moment and focusing on your thoughts, feelings, and sensations. By practicing mindfulness, you can reduce stress, increase focus, and improve your overall well-being.

Building a Strong Support Network

Finally, it's important to build a strong support network to help you navigate the challenges of starting a business. A strong support network can provide you with emotional support, practical help, and a sounding board for your ideas.

Your support network can include friends, family, mentors, and other entrepreneurs. It's important to build a diverse network, with people from different backgrounds and experiences, to give you a broad perspective.

Having a strong support network can also help you stay accountable and motivated. By sharing your goals and progress with others, you'll be more likely to stay on track and achieve your objectives.

Conclusion

Starting a business is full of challenges and obstacles, but with the right mindset and support, you can overcome anything that comes your way. Remember to develop a growth mindset, be persistent, handle rejection, manage stress, and build a strong support network. By following these principles, you'll be able to navigate the obstacles and stay resilient as you build and grow your startup.

It's also important to keep a positive outlook and maintain a sense of humor. Starting a business can be a long and challenging journey, but it's also one of the most rewarding experiences you can have. By staying positive and having a sense of humor, you'll be better equipped to handle adversity and stay motivated.

Finally, it's important to seek help when you need it. Whether it's reaching out to a mentor or therapist, seeking professional advice, or simply talking to friends and family, don't be afraid to ask for help. Building a successful startup is not a one-person job, and seeking help from others is a sign of strength, not weakness.

In conclusion, overcoming adversity is a critical part of the entrepreneurial journey. By staying resilient, developing a growth mindset, and building a strong support network, you'll be able to navigate the challenges and stay motivated as you build and grow your startup. Remember to stay focused, stay positive, and never give up!

Chapter 3: Finding Your Purpose - Defining Your Why and Staying Motivated

Starting a business is more than just a financial pursuit - it's also an opportunity to make a positive impact in the world and find fulfillment in your work. To build a successful startup, you need to be motivated by something greater than money - you need to have a purpose.

In this chapter, we'll explore how to find your purpose, and how to use it to stay motivated and focused as you build your startup.

Defining Your Why

The first step in finding your purpose is to define your "why." Your "why" is the reason you're starting your business - it's what drives you and motivates you to keep going when things get tough.

Your "why" can be personal, such as wanting to spend more time with your family or make a difference in the world. Or it can be more focused on your business, such as wanting to solve a particular problem or create a new product.

To find your "why," take some time to reflect on your values, beliefs, and goals. Ask yourself what's important to you, what motivates you, and what you want to achieve through your business. Write down your thoughts and keep them somewhere you can see them every day.

Using Your Why to Stay Motivated

Once you've defined your "why," use it to stay motivated and focused as you build your startup. Your "why" can provide you with a source of inspiration and help you stay motivated when things get tough.

When you're feeling discouraged, remind yourself of your "why." Think about the positive impact you want to make in the world, or the problem you want to solve. This will help you stay focused and motivated, even when things get tough.

Another way to use your "why" to stay motivated is to make it a part of your business. Incorporate your "why" into your business strategy, your marketing, and your day-to-day operations. This will help you stay aligned with your purpose, and ensure that your business is a reflection of your values and beliefs.

Building a Business with Purpose

Having a purpose is not just about staying motivated - it's also about building a business with meaning and impact. When you build a business with purpose, you're not just creating a product or a service, you're creating something that can make a positive impact in the world.

To build a business with purpose, start by identifying a problem or need that you're passionate about. Then, think about how you can use your business to solve that problem or meet that need.

For example, if you're passionate about environmental sustainability, you might consider starting a business that helps people reduce their carbon footprint, or one that provides environmentally friendly products and services.

When you build a business with purpose, you'll be more likely to attract customers and employees who share your values and beliefs. You'll also be more likely to create a positive impact in the world and find fulfillment in your work.

Staying True to Your Purpose

Finally, it's important to stay true to your purpose as you grow your business. As your business grows, it can be easy to get sidetracked and lose sight of your "why." But if you stay true to your purpose, you'll be more likely to achieve your goals and make a positive impact in the world.

To stay true to your purpose, regularly check in with your "why." Remind yourself of what motivated you to start your business, and make sure that your actions and decisions align with your purpose.

You can also stay true to your purpose by building a culture of purpose in your company. Encourage your employees to understand and embrace your purpose, and make sure that it's woven into everything you do.

Incorporating purpose-driven activities, such as volunteering, into your company culture can also help you stay true to your purpose. By giving back to the community and making a positive impact, you'll be able to stay connected to your purpose and stay motivated as you grow your business.

Finally, seek out partners and investors who share your values and purpose. Working with others who share your vision will help you stay motivated and focused, and ensure that your business stays true to its purpose.

In conclusion, finding your purpose is critical to building a successful and fulfilling startup. By defining your "why," using it to stay motivated, building a business with purpose, and staying true to your purpose, you'll be able to achieve your goals and make a positive impact in the world.

Chapter 4: Building a Strong Team - Finding and Retaining Top Talent

Building a successful startup requires more than just having a great idea - it also requires a strong team. Having the right people in the right roles is critical to achieving your goals and scaling your business.

In this chapter, we'll explore the key steps to building a strong team, from finding and attracting top talent, to retaining and developing your employees.

Finding Top Talent

The first step in building a strong team is to find the right people. But how do you find top talent in a competitive job market?

Start by clearly defining the roles you need to fill and the skills and experience you're looking for in each role. This will help you identify the right candidates and avoid wasting time on resumes that don't fit your requirements.

Next, use a variety of recruitment channels to reach potential candidates. This might include job boards, employee referrals, social media, or professional networking sites. Consider offering incentives, such as referral bonuses, to encourage your employees to refer their friends and colleagues.

When interviewing candidates, don't just focus on their skills and experience - also pay attention to their values, culture fit, and motivation. You want to find people who are not only qualified, but who also share your values and are motivated by your purpose.

Finally, once you've found the right candidates, make sure you're offering competitive salaries and benefits to attract and retain top talent.

Retaining Top Talent

Once you've found top talent, the next step is to retain them. The best way to do this is to create a positive and supportive work environment that encourages your employees to grow and thrive.

Start by setting clear expectations and goals for your employees, and providing them with the resources and support they need to succeed.

Offer regular feedback and coaching to help them grow and develop, and recognize and reward their contributions.

Another important factor in retaining top talent is creating a positive company culture. This means creating a work environment that's inclusive, respectful, and supportive, and fostering a sense of community among your employees.

Developing Your Team

Developing your team is key to building a strong and effective team. It's not enough to just hire the right people - you also need to invest in their growth and development.

One way to develop your team is to provide them with training and professional development opportunities. This might include in-person workshops, online courses, or mentorship programs. Investing in your employees' growth will help them improve their skills, stay motivated, and achieve their full potential.

Another way to develop your team is to provide them with opportunities for growth within the company. Offer promotions, stretch assignments, and cross-functional projects to help your employees expand their skills and responsibilities.

Finally, encourage your employees to share their ideas and provide regular feedback. This will help you identify areas for improvement and create a more innovative and collaborative work environment.

In conclusion, building a strong team is critical to the success of your startup. By finding and retaining top talent, developing your team, and creating a positive and supportive work environment, you'll be able to build a high-performing team that can help you achieve your goals and scale your business.

Chapter 5: Overcoming Challenges and Staying Resilient

Building a successful startup is never a smooth ride. There will be ups and downs, and you'll face a number of challenges along the way.

In this chapter, we'll explore some of the common challenges startups face, and provide strategies for overcoming them and staying resilient.

Managing Stress and Burnout

One of the biggest challenges startups face is stress and burnout. When you're starting a business, you'll be working long hours, dealing with uncertainty and risk, and managing a high level of stress.

To avoid burnout, it's important to take care of your physical and mental health. This might mean setting aside time for exercise, meditation, or other self-care activities. It's also important to set boundaries and limit your working hours, to avoid overworking and burnout.

Another way to manage stress and burnout is to seek support from friends, family, or a mentor. Talking to someone who understands the challenges you're facing can help you gain perspective and find solutions to your problems.

Managing Risk and Uncertainty

Starting a business is inherently risky, and you'll face a number of uncertainties along the way. Whether it's economic uncertainty, competition, or a lack of resources, you'll need to be able to manage risk and uncertainty if you want to succeed.

One way to manage risk is to conduct market research and gather data to inform your decisions. This will help you make informed decisions and reduce the risk of failure.

Another way to manage risk is to create a contingency plan. This means planning for potential risks and having a backup plan in case things don't go as expected.

Finally, it's important to have a strong support network to help you manage risk and uncertainty. Surround yourself with people who believe in your vision and are willing to support you through tough times.

Staying Focused and Motivated

Starting a business can be incredibly rewarding, but it can also be frustrating and disheartening at times. It's important to stay focused and motivated if you want to achieve your goals.

One way to stay focused is to set clear goals and track your progress. This will help you stay motivated and avoid getting distracted by other tasks.

Another way to stay focused is to surround yourself with positive, supportive people. This might mean working with a mentor, forming a support group, or seeking out like-minded individuals who share your vision.

Finally, it's important to celebrate your successes and reward yourself for your hard work. Whether it's taking a day off, treating yourself to a special meal, or just taking some time to relax and recharge, recognizing your achievements will help you stay motivated and focused.

In conclusion, overcoming challenges and staying resilient is key to the success of your startup. By managing stress and burnout, managing risk and uncertainty, and staying focused and motivated, you'll be able to achieve your goals and build a successful business.

In addition to the strategies mentioned above, it's also important to maintain a growth mindset. A growth mindset is the belief that your abilities and intelligence can be developed through hard work, dedication, and learning. When you have a growth mindset, you're more likely to see challenges as opportunities for growth and learning, rather than as obstacles.

Another way to stay resilient is to build resilience habits into your daily routine. This might mean taking time each day to reflect on your accomplishments, focusing on the positive aspects of your life, or engaging in self-care activities like exercise or meditation.

It's also important to have a sense of purpose and meaning. When you're starting a business, it's easy to get caught up in the day-to-day tasks and lose sight of the bigger picture. By focusing on your purpose and the impact you want to make, you'll be able to stay motivated and focused, even when the going gets tough.

It's important to maintain a positive outlook and a sense of perspective. This means avoiding negative self-talk, looking for the good in every situation, and finding humor and joy in the challenges you face. When you're able to maintain a positive outlook, you'll be better equipped to handle the ups and downs of building a startup.

In conclusion, building resilience is an ongoing process that requires effort and dedication. By developing a growth mindset, building resilience habits, focusing on your purpose, and maintaining a positive outlook, you'll be better equipped to handle the challenges that come with starting a business.

Chapter 6: Developing a Growth Mindset: Embracing Change and Continuous Learning

One of the most important qualities of successful entrepreneurs is their ability to continuously grow and adapt to change. This is where the concept of a growth mindset comes into play. The concept of a growth mindset is the idea that skills and intelligence can be improved and expanded through persistent effort and education. In contrast, a fixed mindset is the belief that one's abilities are predetermined and cannot be changed.

Adopting a growth mindset is crucial for entrepreneurs because the business world is constantly evolving, and those who can keep pace with the changes are more likely to succeed. A growth mindset enables entrepreneurs to view challenges and obstacles as opportunities for growth and learning, rather than as insurmountable barriers. It also fosters a desire for continuous improvement and a willingness to take risks and try new things.

So, how can entrepreneurs cultivate a growth mindset? Here are some tips:

Embrace failure: Failure is an inevitable part of the entrepreneurial journey, but those with a growth mindset view it as an opportunity to learn and grow. Instead of being discouraged by failure, they embrace it as a valuable part of the process.

Learn from criticism: Constructive criticism can be difficult to hear, but it can also be incredibly valuable in helping entrepreneurs improve their skills and knowledge. Those with a growth mindset view criticism as an opportunity to learn and grow, rather than as a personal attack.

Be open-minded: Entrepreneurs with a growth mindset are open to new ideas and perspectives, and are willing to consider alternative ways of doing things. This helps them stay innovative and creative, even in the face of challenges.

Cultivate a love of learning: Those with a growth mindset have a love of learning and are always seeking new knowledge and skills. They are constantly striving to improve and grow, both personally and professionally.

Surround yourself with supportive people: Surrounding yourself with people who support and encourage your growth can help foster a growth mindset. Seek out mentors, surround yourself with positive, growth-oriented individuals, and join groups or organizations that align with your entrepreneurial goals.

In conclusion, developing a growth mindset is an ongoing process that requires effort and commitment. But the benefits of embracing change and continuous learning are immense. Entrepreneurs with a growth mindset are more resilient, more innovative, and more likely to succeed in the long run. So, make a conscious effort to cultivate a growth mindset and watch your entrepreneurial journey take flight.

Chapter 7: Creating a Strong Company Culture: Fostering Employee Satisfaction and Loyalty

Company culture is a critical component of a successful business. A strong company culture not only attracts top talent, but it also fosters employee satisfaction, loyalty, and productivity. Entrepreneurs who are able to create a positive and supportive work environment are more likely to achieve their goals and build a successful business.

So, how can entrepreneurs create a strong company culture? Here are some tips:

Define your values and mission: Start by defining your company's values and mission. Make sure they are consistent with your business goals and align with the expectations of your employees. This will help set the tone for your company culture and provide a foundation for decision-making.

Foster open communication: Encourage open and transparent communication between employees and management. This includes regular check-ins, feedback sessions, and opportunities for employees to share their ideas and suggestions. This can help build trust and ensure everyone is working towards a common goal.

Provide opportunities for growth and development: Invest in your employees by providing opportunities for growth and development. Offer training and professional development programs, and encourage employees to pursue new challenges and opportunities within the company.

Recognize and reward employees: Recognize and reward employees for their hard work and contributions. Whether it's through bonuses, promotions, or simply acknowledging their accomplishments, it's important to show your employees that their efforts are valued and

Chapter 8: Scaling Your Business: Strategies for Growth and Expansion

As your startup begins to grow, you'll need to start thinking about how to scale your business in order to continue to drive growth and increase market share. Scaling your business can be a complex and challenging process, but with the right strategy in place, you can turn your startup into a successful and thriving company.

Here are some key strategies for scaling your business:

Focus on efficiency: As your business grows, it's important to focus on efficiency in order to maintain profitability and keep costs under control. Consider implementing new technologies and systems to streamline your operations, and look for ways to automate processes where possible.

Expand your product offering: One of the best ways to drive growth is to expand your product offering. Consider launching new products or services, or entering new markets. This can help you reach new customers and increase your revenue.

Diversify your revenue streams: Diversifying your revenue streams can help reduce your risk and increase your stability. Look for ways to diversify your offerings, whether that's through new products, services, or even new business models.

Invest in marketing and advertising: As you expand, it's important to invest in marketing and advertising in order to reach new customers and increase brand awareness. Consider a combination of traditional and digital marketing strategies, and make sure your messaging is consistent and compelling.

Hire the right team: As your business grows, it's important to have the right team in place to support your growth. Hire top talent, and invest in employee training and development to ensure your team is equipped to handle the challenges and opportunities of a growing business.

Seek out partnerships and collaborations: Finally, consider seeking out partnerships and collaborations to help you scale your business. This can include strategic alliances, joint ventures, or even mergers and acquisitions. Look for opportunities to work with complementary businesses, and consider how these partnerships can help you reach new customers and grow your business.

In conclusion, scaling your business requires a strategic approach and careful planning. By focusing on efficiency, expanding your product offering, diversifying your revenue streams, investing in marketing and advertising, hiring the right team, and seeking out partnerships and collaborations, you can create a successful and thriving business.

Chapter 9: Nurturing a Culture of Innovation: Fostering Creativity and Encouraging Disruptive Thinking

As a startup founder, you want to foster a culture of innovation in order to stay ahead of the competition and continuously drive growth. By nurturing a culture of innovation, you can encourage creativity, spur new ideas, and drive disruptive thinking that will keep your startup ahead of the curve.

Here are some key strategies for nurturing a culture of innovation in your startup:

Encourage open communication and collaboration: Encourage open communication and collaboration among your team members. Create opportunities for employees to share their ideas and work together to find solutions to challenges. This can lead to new and innovative thinking that drives growth.

Foster creativity: Encourage your team to think creatively and explore new and unconventional ideas. Consider hosting brainstorming sessions, encouraging experimentation, and rewarding creative thinking.

Provide resources and support: Make sure your team has access to the resources and support they need to bring their ideas to life. This can include funding, training, and mentorship programs.

Empower employees: Empower your employees to make decisions and take ownership of their work. Encourage risk-taking and experimentation, and provide support and guidance when needed.

Celebrate successes: Celebrate the successes of your team and recognize their contributions. This can help build morale, create a positive work environment, and encourage continued innovation.

Create a flexible work environment: Create a flexible work environment that allows employees to be productive and creative. Consider offering flexible schedules, remote work options, and other perks that help employees feel valued and supported.

Stay current on industry trends: Stay current on industry trends and new technologies. This can help you identify new opportunities for growth and innovation, and keep your startup ahead of the curve.

In conclusion, nurturing a culture of innovation is essential for the success and growth of your startup. By encouraging open communication and collaboration, fostering creativity, providing resources and support, empowering employees, celebrating successes, creating a flexible work environment, and staying current on industry trends, you can create a work environment that fosters innovation and drives growth.

Chapter 10: Staying Focused and On-Track: Balancing Priorities and Managing Time

As a startup founder, it can be easy to get pulled in different directions, especially as your company grows and you take on more responsibilities. However, staying focused and on-track is essential for achieving your goals and driving success. In this chapter, we will explore strategies for balancing your priorities and managing your time effectively.

Set clear goals: Start by setting clear, measurable goals for your business and for yourself. This will help you stay focused on what's important and prioritize your time and efforts accordingly.

Make a plan: Create a plan for achieving your goals, including a timeline and specific action steps. This will help you stay on track and make progress towards your goals.

Prioritize tasks: Make a to-do list and prioritize tasks based on their level of importance and urgency. Focus on the most important tasks first and delegate or outsource tasks that can be done by someone else.

Avoid distractions: Minimize distractions, such as checking your email or social media, during the workday. Instead, set aside specific times for checking email and social media, and stick to it.

Manage your time effectively: Use time management tools and techniques, such as the Pomodoro technique, to help you stay focused and maximize your productivity. Also, be mindful of how you're spending your time, and eliminate any activities or distractions that are not helping you achieve your goals.

Take breaks: Taking breaks is important for your mental and physical well-being. Make time for physical activity, mindfulness practices, or simply taking a few minutes to relax and recharge.

Delegate and outsource: As your startup grows, it may become increasingly difficult to manage all of the tasks on your own. Consider delegating tasks to team members or outsourcing tasks to a freelancer or virtual assistant.

In conclusion, staying focused and on-track is essential for achieving your goals and driving success. By setting clear goals, making a plan, prioritizing tasks, avoiding distractions, managing your time effectively, taking breaks, and delegating and outsourcing, you can stay focused and achieve success. Remember, it's important to strike a balance between work and life, and make time for the things that matter most to you.

Summary

Chapter 1: "Discovering Your Why: Finding Purpose and Meaning in Your Startup Journey"

In this chapter, we explored the importance of having a clear sense of purpose and meaning in your entrepreneurial journey. By focusing on why you started your business, you'll be able to stay motivated and overcome the challenges that come with starting a company. In addition, having a strong sense of purpose can also help you navigate the emotional pressure that can arise during the startup process. The ups and downs of entrepreneurship can be overwhelming at times, but by staying focused on your why, you'll be better able to manage your emotions and stay on track.

Chapter 2: "Embracing a Growth Mindset: Developing Your Skills and Abilities"

This chapter focused on the importance of having a growth mindset as an entrepreneur. A growth mindset involves the belief that your skills and intelligence can be developed through hard work and learning. By embracing a growth mindset, you'll be able to see challenges as opportunities for growth and learning, rather than as obstacles. This can also help you handle the emotional pressure that comes with starting a business. The fear of failure and uncertainty can be overwhelming, but with a growth mindset, you'll be better able to view these challenges as opportunities to grow and improve, rather than as roadblocks.

Chapter 3: "Building Resilience Habits: Staying Motivated and Focused"

In this chapter, we discussed the importance of building resilience habits into your daily routine. This includes taking time to reflect on your accomplishments, focusing on the positive aspects of your life, and engaging in self-care activities. By incorporating resilience habits into your daily life, you'll be better equipped to handle the challenges that come with starting a business, as well as the emotional pressure that can arise during the process. Regular self-reflection and self-care can help you maintain a healthy balance, both emotionally and mentally.

Chapter 4: "Maintaining a Positive Outlook: Finding Joy and Humor in Challenges"

In this chapter, we discussed the importance of maintaining a positive outlook as an entrepreneur. This involves avoiding negative self-talk, looking for the good in every situation, and finding humor and joy in the challenges you face. By maintaining a positive outlook, you'll be better able to handle the ups and downs of building a startup, as well as the emotional pressure that can come with it. Keeping a positive perspective can help you stay motivated and focused, even in the face of adversity.

Chapter 5: "Staying Resilient: An Ongoing Process"

In this chapter, we summarized the key takeaways from the previous chapters and emphasized the importance of building resilience as an ongoing process. This requires effort, dedication, and the development of a growth mindset, resilience habits, a sense of purpose and meaning, and a positive outlook. By incorporating these strategies into your life, you'll be better equipped to navigate the challenges of entrepreneurship and achieve success in your startup journey, as well as handle the emotional pressure that comes with it. Building resilience is a continual process, and requires regular effort and dedication to maintain.

Chapter 6: "Developing a Growth Mindset: Embracing Change and Continuous Learning"

In this chapter, the focus is on the importance of developing a growth mindset in order to succeed as a startup. A growth mindset is the belief that one's abilities and intelligence can be developed through hard work, dedication, and learning. The chapter will explain the benefits of having a growth mindset and provide tips on how to cultivate this mindset in yourself and your team. This will involve embracing change and being open to new ideas, continuously learning and seeking out new opportunities, and being willing to take risks. By developing a growth mindset, entrepreneurs will be better equipped to navigate the challenges and opportunities that come with starting and growing a business.

Chapter 7: "Establishing Your Brand: Defining Your Unique Identity and Value Proposition"

In this chapter, the focus is on establishing a strong brand identity for your startup. A brand is much more than just a logo or tagline - it is the promise you make to your customers and the essence of what makes your business unique. This chapter will cover the steps involved in defining your unique identity, including researching your target market, understanding your competition, and defining your value proposition. The chapter will also offer advice on creating a consistent brand image and voice, both online and offline, in order to build a strong brand that sets you apart from the competition.

Chapter 8: "Strategizing for Success: Creating a Winning Business Plan"

This chapter is all about creating a successful business plan. A well-crafted business plan is essential for any startup, providing a roadmap for success and a tool for securing funding. This chapter will cover the key elements of a business plan, including market research, competition analysis, product and service descriptions, marketing and sales strategies, and financial projections. The chapter will also provide guidance on how to present your plan in the best possible light, both in person and in written form, in order to secure the funding you need to get your business off the ground.

Chapter 9: "Securing Funding: Finding the Right Investors and Maximizing Resources"

In this chapter, the focus is on securing the funding necessary to start and grow your business. The chapter will explore the various options for securing funding, including traditional loans, venture capital, crowdfunding, and more. The chapter will provide advice on how to find the right investors, including how to make a pitch and how to negotiate the best terms. The chapter will also provide tips on how to maximize resources, including how to get the most out of limited funds and how to manage cash flow.

Chapter 10: "Embracing Failure: Learning from Mistakes and Moving Forward"

In this chapter, the focus is on the importance of embracing failure as a part of the entrepreneurial journey. Despite the best-laid plans and the most well-executed strategies, every startup will experience setbacks and failures along the way. This chapter will provide advice on how to view failures as opportunities to learn and grow, rather than as obstacles to success. The chapter will also provide tips on how to overcome setbacks, including how to reframe failures as opportunities for growth, how to learn from mistakes, and how to move forward with resilience and determination. By embracing failure, entrepreneurs will be better equipped to handle the ups and downs of starting and growing a business.

Final Message from the Author

I am deeply committed to sharing my journey and the lessons I have learned with you through this book. My hope is that it will serve as a cornerstone in your own entrepreneurial story, one that is full of beauty, excitement, and purpose. I poured my heart and soul into every page, carefully crafting each word to ensure that it not only provides valuable insights but also inspires and motivates you to take action. I strongly believe that with the right guidance, anyone can turn their dreams into a reality and I am confident that this book will provide that guidance for you. So, I implore you to read it with an open mind, a receptive heart, and a willingness to learn. Embrace the challenges, overcome the obstacles, and never give up on your dreams. Remember, the beauty of entrepreneurship lies in the journey and the experiences it offers. So, embark on this journey with courage and determination, and may this book play a significant role in making your entrepreneurial story one of the most beautiful and exciting ones.

So go forth, take the leap, and never stop chasing your entrepreneurial dreams, for they hold the potential to bring you both personal and professional fulfillment, and create a positive impact on the world around you.

www.ingramcontent.com/pod-product-compliance
Lightning Source LLC
Chambersburg PA
CBHW070322220526
45465CB00013B/2152